1000 African Heroes

Research Booklet

Dallys-Tom Medali

1000 AFRICAN HEROES

ISBN 978-1-947838-09-3

###

###

Solara Editions
New York, Paris, Cotonou

###

Cover Design: Dallys-Tom Medali

###

––––––––––––

Women, Men, Queens, Kings,
Emperors, Presidents, Statesmen,
Martyrs, Inventors, Entrepreneurs,
Artists, Scientists, Athletes, Leaders,
Visionaries, Activists, Farmers,
Educators, Physicians, Magnates,
Philanthropists, Writers, Producers,
Musicians, Founders, Explorers,
Pioneers, Immortals, Heroes.

––––––––––––

To Andrew and Athena, my children.

Foreword

The purpose of this book is to inspire children, teens and even adults. As a young dad, I needed tools to motivate and guide my children, to instill in them enough confidence, positivity and tenacity. There were hardly any books presenting a large selection of illustrious Africans along with how they changed the world and added value for their community or for humanity as a whole. Lilian Thuram's "Mes étoiles noires" took a step in that direction and presented the lives of a handful of models and heroes, but I still needed more. I needed a wider selection from all walks of life. Whatever a child's dream, it's important to have precursors and role-models that he or she can emulate. This is what this book is trying to offer.

The project took two years of research, compilation and writing. At first, the book took the form of an encyclopedia with the maximum of useful details provided on each featured individual. But half way through, I switched to the format of a research notebook or booklet. Under this format, just one or two lines of information are offered on each individual and an additional empty space is reserved so that users of the book (ideally a young adult or a child assisted by an adult) can research his favorite heroes' journey and achievements, and fill in the gaps. The exercise becomes participatory and the reader is more engaged and better inspired.

All the entries are classified on first name (and sometimes nickname) basis, instead of the classic habit or sorting based on surname (or family name). This will make the content and all the heroes even more accessible.

A hero is a person admired or idealized for his courage, his service, his excellent achievements or his noble qualities; regardless of race, ethnicity, age, gender, religion, ideology and background. The book features black African heroes, white African heroes, Aboriginal heroes and heroes from the Diaspora, whether they live or have lived in Africa, Oceania, Europe, Asia or America.

Norbert Zongo, an African journalist and martyr once wrote: "Life is short, the life of heroes is even shorter." I hope this book will give you enough inspiration to live the best possible version of your life.

A

Abédi Ayew Pélé (1964 - Present), footballer

Abla Pokou (1730-1750), queen of Cote d'Ivoire

Abubakar Tafawa Balewa (1912 – 1966), statesman

Achille Mbembe (1957 - Present), philosopher

Adam Clayton Powell Jr (1908-1972), pastor and politician

Adandozan Madogugu (x-1861), king of Dahomey

Addi Ba Mamadou (1916-1943), anti-colonial activist, fighter for the liberation of France

Adjahouto Agassou (x-x), patriarch of the kings of Dahomey

Adolphus Hailstork (1941-present), composer

Agadja Dossou (1673-1740), king of Dahomey

Agoli Agbo (1850-1940), king of Dahomey

Agoli Agbo Dedjalagni (x-2018), king of Abomey

Agonglo (1766-1797), king of Dahomey

Ahmad Baba al-Abbas al-Massufi al-Tinbukti (1556-1627), philosopher and leader

Ahmad Musa (1992-present), footballer

Ahmadou Kourouma (1927-2003), writer

Ahmed Hassan Zewail (1946-2016), Nobel Prize in chemistry and father of femto-chemistry

Ahmed Sékou Touré (1922-1984), statesman, pan-africanist and first president of Guinea

Aime Césaire (1913-2008), poet

Akaba Houessou (x-1716), king of Dahomey

Akhenaton d'Egypte (x-1334BC), legendary pharaoh

Akon Aliaume Damala Thiam (1973-present), musician and entrepreneur

Al Green (1946), musician

Alain Towedo Capo-Chichi (1978-present), teacher and entrepreneur

Alain Mabanckou (1966-present), writer

Alan Paton (1903-1988), writer

Albert Elea Namatjira (1902-1959), aboriginal artist

Albert Luthuli (1898-1967), teacher, activist and Nobel peace prize laureate

Alberta A. Ollennu (x-x), writer

Alberta Williams King (1904-1974), activist and mother of MLK.

Alex Haley (1921-1992), writer

Alexandre Miles (1838-1918), inventor

Alexandre Pouchkine (1799-1837), legendary Russian writer of African descent

Alexandre Biyidi Awala (Mongo Beti ou Eza Boto) (1932-2001), writer and activist

Alexandria Ocasio-Cortez (1989-present), activist and congresswoman

Alfa Yaya Maudo (1830-1912), king of Labé in Guinea

Alfred-Amédée Dodds (1842-1922), franco-senegalese general and colonialist

Ali Farka Toure (1939-2006), musician

Ali Mazrui (1933-2014), writer

Alia Atkinson (1988-present), swimmer

Alice Walker (1944-present), writer and activist

Aliko Dangote (1957-present), ultra-wealthy businessman

Allan Anthony Donald (1966-present), cricket player

Allen Iverson (1975-present), basketball legend

Allyson Felix (1985-present), legendary athlete

Allyson Kay Duncan (1951-present), judge

Almamy Suluku (1820-1906), powerful king

Alpha Blondy Seydou Koné (1953-present),
musician and activist

Alphadi Sidahmed Seidnaly (1957-present), stylist

Althea Gibson (1927-2003), tennis champion and

activist

Alton Sterling (1979-2016), martyr

Alvin Ailey (1931-1989), choreographer and activist

Alvin Singleton (1940-present), composer

Alvin Slaughter (1955-present), musician and pastor

Ama Ata Aidoo (1942-present), writer

Amadou Bamba (1850-1927), Sufi leader and anti-colonial activist

Amadou Hampate Ba (1901-1991), writer and

ethnologist

Amazons (x-x), legendary women fighters of Dahomey

Amelia Isadora Platts Boynton Robinson (1911-2015), activist

Amenhotep III (x-1351BC), legendary pharaoh

Amilcar Cabral (1924-1973), engineer, statesman and martyr

Amina (x-x), Queen of Nigeria

Aminata Diallo Glez (1972-present), film producer

Aminata Traoré (1942-present), writer

Aminatta Forna (1964-present), writer

Amiri Baraka (1934-2014) writer

Amos Tutuola (1920-1997), writer

Amy Ashwood, (1897-1969), activist

Amy Jacques Garvey (1895-1973), writer and activist

Andre Brink (1935-2015), writer

Andre Matsoua (1899-1942), politician and religious

Andre Watts (1946-present), composer and musician

Andrew Jackson Beard (1849-1921), freed slave, inventor and entrepreneur

Angela Evelyn Bassett (1958-present), actress

Angelique Kidjo (1960-present), musician and activist

Anita Florence Hemmings (1872-1960), pioneer and librarian

Antenor Firmin Joseph Auguste (1850-1911), anthropologist and precursor of the works by Cheikh Anta Diop

Anthony Anderson (1970-present), actor and comedian

Anthony Davis (1951-present), composer and musician

Anthony Davis Marshon Jr (1993-present), basketball player

Anthony Johnson (1984-present), martial artist

Anthony Joshua (1989-present), boxing champion

Anton Wilhelm Amo (Anthony William) (1703-1759), philosopher

Antonio Tavaris Brown Sr (1988-present), American football player

Anwar Sadat (1918-1970), statesman

Archie Roach (1957-present), legendary aboriginal singer

Aretha Franklin (1942-2018), musician and composer

Arlie Petters (1964-present), mathematician and physicist

Arna Bontemps (1902-1973), writer

Arthur Robert Ashe Jr (1943-1993), activist and tennis legend

Arthur Bertram Cuthbert Walker Jr, (1936–2001), astronaut, physicist and inventor

Arthur Beetson (1945-2011), aboriginal star of Australian rugby

Arthur Cunningham (1928-1997), composer

Asamoah Gyan (1985-present), footballer

Aubrey Faulkner (1881-1930), cricket legend

Audre Lorde (1934-1992), writer

August Wilson (1945-2005), composer

Ava DuVernay (1972-present), movie producer

Ayanna Pressley (1974-present), congresswoman

Ayaovi Papavi King Mensah (1971-present), musician

Ayi Kwei Arman (1939-present), writer

————————————

B

Babemba Traore (1855-1898), king

Banduk Marika (1954-present), aboriginal artist

Barack Hussein Obama (1961-present), lawyer, writer and statesman

Barry Lamar Bonds (1964-present), legendary baseball player

Barry Richards (1945-present), cricket player

Barry Sanders (1968-present), American football player

Barry White (1944-2003), musician

Bass Reeves (1838-1910), US marshal in the Wild West, nicknamed "the invincible"

Battling Siki (Louis Mbarick Fall) (1897-1925), boxer

Beatrix McCleary Hamburg (1923-2018), psychiatrist

Behanzin Kondo (1845-1906), king of Dahomey and anti-colonial warrior

Ben Camey Wallace (1974-present), basket baller

Ben Earl King (1938-2015), musician

Ben Okri (1959-present), poet and writer

Benjamin Banneker (1731-1806), writer and naturalist

Benjamin Montgomery (1819-1877), inventor

Benjamin O. Davis Jr (1912-2002), air force general and commander of the Tuskegee corps

Benjamin O. Davis Sr (1877-1970), general of the US army

Benjamin Solomon Carson Sr (1951-present), politician and brilliant neurosurgeon

Bernadette Tyree (x-x), biochemist

Bernandin Gantin (1922-2008), brilliant archbishop and former head of the college of Catholic Cardinals in Rome `

Bernie Mac Bernard Jeffrey McCullough (1957-2008), comedian and actor

Bertha Coombs (1961-present), journalist

Bertin Nahum (1969-present), inventor

Bessie Griffin (Arlette B. Broil) (1914-2009),
musician

Bessie Coleman (1892-1926),first black pilot

Bessie Head (1937-1986), writer

Bessie Smith (1894-1937), musician

Beyonce Gisele Knowles (1981-present) musician

Bill Campbell (1953-present), lawyer, politician,
former mayor of Atlanta

Bill Cosby (1937-present), actor and producer

Bill Russel (1934-present), champion and basketball legend

Billie Holiday Eleanora Fagan (1915-1959), musician

Binyavanga Wainaina (1971-present), journalist and writer

Biya Bandele (1967-present), movie producer and writer

Blaise Galaye Mbaye Diagne (1872–1934), politician

Bo Diddley (1928-2008), singer and musician

Bo Jackson (1962-present), American football player

Bob Marley (1945-1981), legendary musician and king of reggae

Bob Robert Lewis Maza (1939-2000), aboriginal actor

Bobby Brown Robert Barisford (1969-present), musician

Booker Tio Robert Huffman (1965-present), legendary wrestler

Booker Taliaferro Jones Jr (1944-present), musician

Booker T. Washington (1856-1915), brilliant

educator and activist

Boutros Boutros-Ghali (1922-2016), diplomat and politician, former head of the United Nations

Brandy Rayana Norwood (1979-present), singer and actress

Brenda Fassie (1964-2004), musician

Brice Sinsin (1959-present), educator and researcher

Buchi Florence Onyebuchi Emecheta (1944-2017), writer

Buddy Guy (1936-present), legendary musician

C

Caesar Carpentier Antoine (1836–1921), politician

Calestous Juma (1953-2017), educator

California J. Cooper (1931-2014), writer

Calvin Johnson (1985-present), American football player

Camara Laye (1928-1980), writer

Camille Mortenol (1859-1930), military officer

Cara Black (1979-present), tennis player

Carl Lewis (1961-present), legendary athlete and olympic champion

Carlota Lukumi (x-1844), anti-slavery rebel leader

Carmelita Jeter (1979-present), olympic champion

Carol Elisabeth Moseley Braun (1947-present), lawyer, politician, senator and activist

Cathy (Catherine Astrid Salome) Freeman (1973-present), aboriginal olympic champion

Cesaria Evora (1941-2011), singer

Cetshwayo Kampande (1826-1884), Zulu king

Chad Javon Johnson Ochocinco (1978-present), American football player

Charles Bradley (1948-2017), musician

Charles B. Brooks (1865-x), inventor

Charles Drew (1904-1950), inventor

Charles Henry Turner, (1867–1923), zoologist

Charles N'Tchorere (1896-1940), commander and WW2 hero

Charles E. Phillips (1959-preent), CEO and businessman

Charles R. Johnson (1948-present), writer

Charles W Chappelle (1872-1941), inventor and aerospace engineer

Charles Wesley Turnbull (1935-present), politician and former governor of the Virgin Islands

Charles Young (1864–1922), former slave and first black US Army colonel

Charlotte Hawkins Brown (1883-1961), educator and writer

Cheikh Anta Diop (1923-1986), scientist, educator and writer

Cheikh Hamidou Kane (1928-present), writer

Cheikh Modibo Diarra (1952-present), astrophysicist and politician

Chelsea Nichelle Gray (1992-present), basketball player

Cheryl Miller (1964-present), basketball coach

Chester Himes (1909-1984), writer

Chevalier de Saint-Georges (1745-1799), brilliant composer

Chika Unigwe (1974-present), writer

Chimamanda Ngozi Adichie (1977-present), writer

Chinelo Okparanta (1981-present), writer

Chinua Achebe (1930-2013), writer

Chiwetel Umeadi Ejiofor (1977-present), actor

Chris Brown (1989-present), musician

Chris Christopher Julius Rock III (1965-present), comedian

Chris Gardner (1954-present), homeless turned broker and multi-millionnaire philanthropist

Chris Tucker (1971-present), actor

Christian Barnard (1922-2001), legendary surgeon

Christiane Taubira (1952-present), politician and writer

Christine Ijeoma Ohuruogu (1984-present), olympic champion

Christopher Okigbo (1932-1967), writer

Chuck Berry (1926-2017), musician, father of rock-n-roll

Clara Byrd Baker (1886-1979), educator and activist

Clarence Seedorf (1976-present), legendary football player

Clarence Skip Ellis (1943-2014), professor emeritus of computer science

Clarence Thomas (1948-present), American Supreme Court Justice

Claude Steele (1946-present), psychologist and educator

Claudy Siar (1964-present), journalist and musician

Clayton LeBouef (1954-present), actor

Cleopatra VII (70 avant JC-30 avant JC), queen of Egypt

Clifford Possum Tjapaltjarri (1932-2002), aboriginal artist

Coleridge-Taylor Perkinson (1932-2004), composer

Common Lonnie J. S. Rashid Lynn Jr (1972-present), musician

Countee Cullen (1903-1946), writer

Cuba Michael Gooding Jr (1968-present), actor

Cudjoe Oluale Kossola Lewis (1841-1935), last slave in the U.S.

Cudjoe Nanny (1680-1744), Jamaican queen born in Ghana

Curtis Lee Mayfield (1942-1999), legendary musician

Cynthia Cozette Lee (1953-present), composer

Cynthia Lynne Cooper-Dyke (1963-present), basketball legend

Cyprien Tokoudagba (1939-2012), artist, historian and bas-reliefs expert

————————-

D

Dallys Medali (1987-present), writer, CPA and businessman

Dambudzo Marechera (1952-1987), writer

Dana Elaine Owens (Queen Latifah) (1970-present),

actress and musician

Dandara (x-1694), anti-slavery strategist and fighter

Dani Alves (1983-present), Brazilian footballer and champion

Danialou Sagbohan (x-present), musician

Daniel Hale Williams (1856-1931), legendary surgeon

Danny Lebern Glover (1946-present), actor

Darryl A. Williams (x-present), general, first black director of the West Point military academy

Dave David Khari Webber Chappelle (1973-present), comedian,

David Frank Adjaye (1966-present), brilliant architect

David Baker (1931-2016), composer

David Blackwell (1919-2010), statistician

David Crosthwait (1898-1976), engineer

David Gulpilil Dalaithngu (1953-present), dancer, actor and aboriginal leader

David Livingstone (1813-1873), Scottish christian missionary, hero of the fight against slavery

David Medali (1957-present), engineer and preacher

David Robinson (1965-present), basketball legend

David Oyelowo (1976 - present), actor

David Unaipon (1872-1967), prêcheur, auteur and inventor

Dedan Kimathi Waciuri (1920-1957), rebelle and militant anti-colonial

Deion Luywnn Sanders Sr. (1967-present), American football and baseball player

Demarcus Boogie Amir Cousins (1990-present), basketball player

Dennis Keith Rodman (1961-present), basketball legend

Denzel Washington (1954-present), legendary actor

Derrick Rose (1988-present), basketball player

Desmond Tutu (1931-present), archbishop, activist and Nobel peace prize winner

Diana Ross (1944-present), musician

Diana Sands (1934-1973), actress

Didi Waldyr Pereira (1928-2001), football legend

Didier Awadi (1969-present), musician and activist

Didier Yves Tebily Drogba (1978-present), champion and football legend

Dikembe Jean-Jacques Mutombo (1966-present), basketball legend and philanthropist

Dinaw Mengestu (1978-present), writer

Djalma Pereira Dias dos Santos (1929-2013), football legend

Djimon Gaston Hounsou (1964-present), actor

Don Donald Frank Cheadle Jr (1964-present), actor

Dona Beatrice Kimpa Vita (1684-1706), religious leader

Donal Fox (1952-present), composer

Donald Glover McKinley Jr (1983-present), actor

Donna Summer Adrian Gaines (1948-2012), musician

Donny Edward Hathaway (1945-1979), musician

Doris Pilkington Garimara (1937-2014), aboriginal

Dorothy Napangardi (1956-2013), aboriginal artist

Dorothy Peters (1930-present), aboriginal lawyer

Douglas Palmer (1951-present), politician

Dr Dre Andre Romelle Young (1965-present), musician and producer

Drake Aubrey Graham (1986-present), musician

Duke Ellington (1899-1974), musician

Duse Mohamed Ali (1866-1945), actor and politician

_____-

E

Earl Little (1890-1931) & Louise Little (1897-1991),

activists and parents of Malcolm X

Earl Renfroe, (1907–2000), orthodontist

Eddie Kendricks (1939-1992), musician

Eddy Murphy (1961-present), actor and comedian

Edmonia Mary Lewis (1844-1907), legendary sculptor

Eduardo Chivambo Mondlane (1920-1969), anthropologist and independence fighter

Edward Bland (1926-2013), composer

Elbert R. Robinson (x-x), inventor

El Hadji Diouf (1981-present), footballer

El Hadj Omar Tall (1797-1864), political, religious and military leader

Eleanor Taylor Bland (1944-2010), writer

Elgin Gay Baylor (1934-present), basketball legend

Elijah Eugene Cummings (1951-present), politician

Elijah McCoy (1844-1929), engineer and inventor (57 patents)

Elijah Muhammad Robert Poole (1897-1975), religious leader

Elizabeth Keckley (1818-1907), writer

Ella Baker (1903-1986), activist

Ella Fitzgerald (1917-1996), musician

Ellen Johnson Sirleaf (1938 – Present), stateswoman and Nobel peace prize winner

Elon Musk (1971-present), inventor and brilliant South-African entrepreneur

Emily Kame Kngwarreye (1910-1996), aboriginal artist

Emmett Chappelle (1925-present), biochemist

Emmitt James Smith III (1969-present), American football player

Emmett Till (1941-1955), martyr

Endubis (270-300), king of Aksum (currently in Ethiopia and Erythrea)

Eric Garner (1970-2014), martyr

Eric Holder (1951-present), legendary lawyer and US Attorney General under Obama

Erich Jarvis (1965-present), neurobiologist and educator

Ernest Everett Just (1883-1941), biologist

Ernest J. Gaines (1933-present), writer

Ernest J. Wilkins Jr (1923-2011), engineer and nuclear scientist

Ernie Davis (1939-1963), American football player

Ernie Ashley Dingo (1956-present), aboriginal actor

Es'kia Mphahlele (1919-2008), writer

Esope (620 avant JC - 564 avant JC), greek philosopher of African descent

Eugene Jacques Bullard (1895-1961), pioneer and

air force pilot

Eusebio da Silva Ferreira (1942-2014), football legend

Eva Johnson (1946-present), poet and aboriginal actress

Evers Wiley Medgar (1925-1963), activist

Evonne Goolagong Cawley (1951-present), aboriginal tennis legend

Ezana (x-356), king of Aksum (in Ethiopia and Erythrea)

Ezekiel Kemboi (1982-present), olympic champion

F

Fardoll Ezeckiel Medali (1997-present), agronome

Fatou Diome (1968-present), writer

Fats Domino (1928-2017), singer

Fela Anikulapo-Kuti (1938-1997), musician and
activist

Felix Houphouet Boigny (1905-1993), statesman

Felix Konotey-Ahulu (1930-present), brilliant
physician

Felix Kossouoh (x-present), IT engineer

Ferdinand Oyono (1929-2010), writer

Flora Nwapa (1931-1993), writer

Florence B. Price (1887-1953), composer

Forest Whitaker (1961-present), actor

Frank E. Petersen Jr (1932-2015), air force general

Frantz Fanon (1925-1961), writer and psychiatrist

Fred Hampton (1948 - 1969), activist and martyr

Frederick Douglass (1818-1895), abolition leader and writer

Frederick McKinley Jones (1893-1961), inventor and entrepreneur

Frederik De Klerk (1936-present), statesman and Nobel peace prize winner

Freddie Gray (1990-2015), martyr of US police brutality

Freeman Alphonsa Hrabowski III (1950-present), educator and mathematician

—————————-

G

Gabrielle (Gabby) Christina Victoria Douglas (1995-present), gymnast and olympic champion

Gabrielle Union (1972-present), actress

Gael Monfils (1986-present), tennis player

Gamal Abdel Nasser (1918-1970), statesman

Gangnihessou Do Aklin (x-1620), king of Dahomey

Garcelle Beauvais (1966-present), actress

Garrett Morgan (1877-1963), inventor

Garrincha Manoel Francisco dos Santos
(1933-1983), footballer

Gary Foley (1950-present), aboriginal activist

Gary Player (1935-present), golf legend from South Africa

Gaston Monnerville (1897-1991), lawyer and politician

Gawirrin Gumana (1935-present), aboriginal artist

Gayle King (1954-present), TV presenter and editor

George (Iceman) Gervin (1952-present), basketball legend

George Bridgewater (1778-1860), musician

George Edward Alcorn, Jr (1940-present), physicist and inventor

George Franklin Grant (1846-1910), dentist, inventor and first black professor of Harvard

George Foreman (1949-present), boxing legend

George Gershwin (1898-1937), brilliant composer

George Junius Stinney Jr. (1929-1944), martyr

George Padmore (1903-1959), journalist

George Robert Carruthers (1939-present), inventor, physicist and astronaut

George T. Samon (1861-1902), army man and inventor

George Theophilus Walker (1922-present), composer

George Washington Carver (1864-1943), inventor

George Weah Tawlon Manneh Oppong Ousman (1966-present), footballer and statesman

Glele Badohoun (1814-1889), king of Dahomey

Gloria Naylor (1950-2016), writer

Gloria Petyarre (1938-present), aboriginal artist

Gnonnas Pedro (1943-2004), musician

Godfrey Nzamujo (1950-present), agronome and entrepreneur

Gordon Parks (1912-2006), photographer

Graca Machel (1945-present), politician

Graeme Pollock (1944-present), South African cricket legend

Granville Woods, (1856–1910), inventor

Gregory M. Sleet (1951-present), juge

Guezo Gakpe (x-1858), king of Dahomey

Guillaume Guillon (1760-1832), painter

Gwendolyn Brooks (1917-2000), brilliant writer

Guimbi Ouattara (1836-1919), princess and politician

——————————

H

Haile Gebrselassie (1973-present), olympic champion

Haile Selassie (1892-1975), emperor

Hale Smith (1925-2009), composer

Halle Maria Berry (1966-present), actress

Hangbe (x-x), Queen of Dahomey

Hank Aaron (1934-present), baseball legend

Hannibal Abraham Petrovitch (1696-1781), brilliant
engineer, Russian general of African descent

Harold Amos (1918-2003), microbiologist and
Harvard professor

Harold Washington (1922-1987), first black mayor
of Chicago

Harriet Ann Jacobs (1813-1897), writer

Harriet E. Wilson (1825-1900), novelist

Harriet Tubman (1820-1913), activist and anti-slavery hero

Harry Burleigh (1866-1949), composer

Hattie McDaniel (1895-1952), singer and actress

Hector Tjupuru Burton (1937-2017), aboriginal artist

Helen Oyeyemi (1984-present), writer

Helen Suzman (1917-2009), anti-apartheid activist

Helon Habila (1967-present), writer

Hendrik Witbooi (1830-1905), Namibian hero

Henrietta Lacks (1920-1951), gave her cells for worldwide scientific research

Henrietta Vinton Davis (1860-1941), writer

Henry Blair (1807-1860), inventor

Henry Brown (x-x), inventor

Henry McBay (1914-1995), chemist

Heva (x-x), legendary slave and rebel

Hicham El Guerrouj (1974-present), olympic champion

Hildrus Poindexter (1901–1987), bacteriologist and epidemiologist

Hosea Komombumbi Kutako (1870-1970), independence leader in Namibia

Hosea Lorenzo Williams (1926-2000), activist and philanthropist

Houegbadja Aho (x-1685), king of Dahomey

Howard Swanson (1907-1978), composer

Hugh Masekela (1939-2018), musician

I

Ibrahi Njoya (1860-1933), king of Cameroon

Ice Cube O'Shea Jackson Sr (1969-present), musician

Ida B. Wells (1862-1931), journalist and activist

Ida L. Gisele Tokpo (1965-present), engineer and activist for women and children rights

Ilhan Omar (1981-present), congresswoman

Imhotep (x-x), priest, engineer, architect and chancellor of pharaoh Djoser

Ira Aldridge (1807-1867), actor

Ira Gershwin (1896-1983), musician and composer

Isaac Lee Hayes (1942-2008), musician

Isaac R. Johnson (1812-1879), inventor

Isaiah Lord Thomas III (1961-present), basketball legend

Ishmael Scott Reed (1938-present), writer

Ishmael Larry Smith (1988-present), basket-baller

Issa Rae Jo Diop (1985-present), actress and producer

Ivan Gladstone Van Sertima (1935-2009), researcher and writer

––––––––––

J

John Maxwell Coetzee (1940-present), writer and Nobel prize winner

J.B. Danquah (Nana Joseph Kwame Kyeretwie Boakye Danquah) (1895-1965), statesman

J.R.R. Tolkien John Ronald Reuel (1892-1973),

professor and legendary writer

Jackie Joyner Kersee (1962-present), legendary athlete

Jackie Robinson (1919-1972), athlete and activist

Jackie Wilson Jr Jack Leroy (1934-1984), singer

Jacob Desvarieux (1955-present), musician

Jacques Alidou Kousse (x-2018), CPA and auditor

Jada Pinkett Koren Smith (1971-present), actress

Jahana Hayes (1973-present), congresswoman

Jaja de Opobo (1821-1891), king

Jalen Lattrel Ramsey (1994-present), American football player

Jamaica Kincaid (1949-present), writer

James A. Harris (1932-2000), chemist

James Baldwin (1924-1987), writer

James Brown Joseph (1933-2006), brilliant musician

James Emman Kwegyir Aggrey (1875-1927), missionary and teacher

James Leonard Farmer Jr (1920-1999), activist

James Harden (1989-present), basketball player

James Luther Bevel (1936-2008), pastor and activist

James McLurkin (1972-present), robotics engineer

James Sylvester Gates (1950-present), brilliant physicist

James Edward Maceo West (1931-present), inventor,

Jamie Foxx Eric Marlon Bishop (1967-present) musician, actor and comedian

Jan Matzeliger (1852-1889), inventor

Janani Jakaliya Luwum (1922-1977) Archbishop of Uganda

Jane C. Wright (1919–2013), surgeon and researcher

Janet Emerson Bashen (1957-present), inventor and entrepreneur

Janet Damita Jo Jackson (1966-present), singer

Janet Louise Hubert (1956-present), actress

Janvier Assogba (1937-2017), colonel and stateman

Jasmine Plummer (1993-present), female American football player

Jay Jay Augustine Azuka Okocha (1973), football legend

Jay Z (Shawn Corey Carter) (1969-present), musician and producer

Jean Miche Kankan (1956-1997), comedian

Jean-Michel Basquiat (1960-1988), legendary artist

Jean Pliya, (1931-2015) writer

Jean Tommer (1894-1967), writer

Jean-Jacques Dessalines (1758-1806), military general and freedom fighter for Haiti

Jean-Michel Basquiat (1960-1988), legendary artist

Jennifer Kate Hudson (1981-present), singer and actress

Jerome Heartwell "Brud" Holland (1916–1985), educator

Jerome Fagla Medegan (x-present), inventor and researcher

Jerome O. Nriagu (1944-present), geochemist

Jerry Lawson (1940-2011), IT engineer

Jerry John Rawlings (1947-present), army captain and statesman

Jerry Lee Rice (1962-present), American football player

Jesse Louis Jackson Sr (1941-present), activist and politician

Jesse Owens (1913-1980), legendary athlete and olympic champion

Jesse Eugene Russell (1948-present), engineer and inventor

Jim Brown James Nathaniel (1936-present),

legendary sportsman

Jimi Hendrix (1942-1970), legendary musician

Jimmy Butler (1989-present), basketball player

Jimmy Chi James Ronald (1948-2017), aboriginal musician

Jimmy Little James Oswald (1937-2012), aboriginal musician

Jocelyne Beroard (1954-present), musician

Joe Louis Joseph Barrow (1914-1981), legendary boxer

John Albert Burr (x-x), inventor

John Boyega Adebayo Adegboyega (1992-present), actor

John Chilembwe (1871-1915), pastor and educator

John E. Hodge (1914-1996), chemist

John Edgar Widerman (1941-present), writer

John Hendrik Clarke (1915-1998), historian and writer

John Lee Love (1889-1931), inventor

John Hamilton McWhorter (1965-present), linguist

and creole language expert

John Mensah Sarbah (1864-1910), lawyer and statesman

John Pepper J.P. Clark Bekederemo (1935-present), writer

John Standard (1868-x), inventor

John T. Biggers (1924–2001), artist

John Uzo Ogbu (1939-2003), anthropologist

Johnny Bulunbulun (1946-2010), aboriginal artist

Jomo Kenyatta (1897-1978), statesman and first

president of Kenya

Joseph Bileou Oschoffa (1909-1985), prophet and church founder

Joseph Ki-Zerbo (1922-2006), brilliant historian

Joseph L. Graves (1955-present), nano-biologist and professor

Joseph H. Smith (x-x), inventor

Josephine Mary Premice (1926-2001), singer and actress

Joshua Nkomo Mqabuko Nyongolo (1917-1999), statesman

Josiah Henson (1789-1883), writer and abolitionist

Joyce Banda (1950 - present), former president of Zambia

Julia C. Collins (1842-1865), writer and educator

Julia Perry (1924-1979), composer

Julian Francis Abele (1881-x), brilliant architect

Julius Eastman (1940-1990), composer

Julius Nyerere Kambarage (1922-1999), statesman

Jupiter Hammon (1720-1800), poet, activist and former slave

Justin Gatlin (1982-present), olympic champion

Justine Hountondji (x-present), religious sister

Justine Saunders (1953-2007), aboriginal actress

————————————

K

Kalusha Bwalya (1963-present), legendary football player

Kankan Mansa Musa (1280-1337), leader of the wealthy ancient Malian empire

Kara Walker (1969-present), artist

Kareem Abdul Jabbar (1947-present), basketball legend

Katherine Johnson, (1918-present) mathematician and physicist for NASA

Kawhi Leonard (1991-present), basketball player

Kayne West (1977-present), musician , designer and producer

Keke Palmer Keyana Lauren (1993-present), actress and singer

Kelly Miller (1863-1939), scientist

Kémi Séba (Stellio Gilles Robert Capo Chichi) (1981-present), activist

Ken Saro Wiwa (1941-1995), activist and writer

Kenenisa Bekele (1982-present), olympic champion

Kenneth Frazier (1954-present), CEO of a pharmaceutical multinational company

Kenneth Irvine Chenault (1951-present), CEO of the Fortune 500 company American Express

Kenneth Kaunda (1924-present), statesman and first president of Zambia

Kerrie Lamont Holley (1954-present), IT engineer

Kerry Marisa Washington (1977-present), actress

Kevin Anderson (1986-present), South-African tennis player

Kevin Clash (1960-present), legendary puppeteer

Kevin Durant (1988-present), basketball legend

Kevin Gilbert (1933-1993), aboriginal writer

Kevin Hart (1979-present), comedian

Khaled Adenon (1985-present), footballer

Khalil Delshon Mack (1991-present), American football player

Kobe Bryant (1978-present), basketball legend

Kofi Atta Annan (1938-2018), legendary diplomat, former head of the UN, Nobel Peace Prize winner

Kofi Awoonor (1935-2013), writer

Kofi Osei Tutu I (1660-1717), king of Ghana

Kpengla (x-1789), king of Dahomey

Kunle Ayinde Olukotun (x-present), IT engineer, teacher and entrepreneur

Kwabena Boahen (1964-present), engineer and professor

Kwame Nkrumah (1909-1972), statesman

Kylian Mbappe (1998-present), footballer and world champion

––––––––––

L

Laila Ali (1977-present), boxing champion

Lamine Gueye (1891-1968), politician

Langston Hughes (1901-1967), activist, poet and novelist

LaShawn Merritt (1986-present), olympic champion

Lat Jor Dior Ngone Latip (1842-1886), king

Lauren Simmons (1995-present), trader on the New York Stock Exchange

Laurence Fishburn (1961-present), actor and producer

Lawrence Taylor (1959-present), American football player

Lebron James (1984-present), basketball legend

Lecba Elizier Cadet (1897-x), activist and vaudou priest

Lee Burridge (1861-1915), inventor

Lee Raphael Carl (1949-present), surgeon, engineer and entrepreneur

Lee Stiff (1949-present), mathematician and educator

Leila Aboulela (1964-present), writer

Leon Bates (1949-present), composer and musician

Leonidas Berry (1902-1995), physician

Leopold Sedar Senghor (1906-2001), poet and statesman

Leslie Adams (1932-present), classical composer

Leslie Jones (1967-present), comedian and actress

Leslie Odom Jr (1981-present), actor and musician

Leslie Garland Bolling (1898–1955), artist

Lewis Adams (1842-1905), educator

Lewis Hamilton (1985-present), driving legend and Formula 1 champion

Lewis Howard Latimer (1848-1928), inventor

Lewis Temple, (1800–1854), inventor

Leymah Roberta Gbowee (1972-present), activist and Nobel Peace Prize winner

Lilian Thuram Ruddy Ulien (1972-present), footballer and champion

Lincoln Walter Hawkins (1911-1992), lawyer, inventor and educator

Lionel Ritchie Brockman Jr (1949-present), legendary musician

Lionel Rose Edmund (1948-2011), aboriginal boxing champion

Lisa Deshaun Leslie (1972-present), basketball legend

Liz Elizabeth Cambage (1991-present), basketball player

Lloyd Albert Quarterman, (1918–1982) chemist

Lloyd Augustus Hall (1894-1971), chemist and inventor with 59 patents

Lloyd P. Ray (1860-1940), inventor

Lonnie George Johnson (1949-present), inventor and engineer with 120 patents

Lonnie Walker IV (1998-present), basketball player

Lorraine Hansberry (1930-1965), actor

Louis Armstrong Daniel (1901-1971), legendary musician

Louis Delgres (1772-1802), military officer and freedom fighter for Guadeloupe

Louis Farrakhan Sr (1933-present), activist

Louis T. Wright (1891–1952), surgeon

Lowitja Lois O'Donoghue (1932-present), aboriginal activist

Luambo Luanzo Makiadi Francois (Franco) (1938-1989), legendary musician

Lucky Philip Dube (1964-2007), legendary musician

Lucy (x-x), prehistoric fossile, symbolic mother of all humans

——————————-

M

Madam CJ Walker (1867-1919), entrepreneur and inventor

Madison Keys (1995-present), tennis player

Mae C. Jemison (1956-present), astronaut and engineer

Magic Earvin Johnson Jr (1959-present), legendary basketball player

Major Taylor Marshall Walter (1878-1932),

legendary cyclist

Malcolm Gladwell (1963-present), writer and journalist

Malcolm X (1925-1965), activist and martyr

Mandawuy D. Yunupingu (1956-2013), aboriginal singer

Manu Dibango Emmanuel N'Djoke (1933-present), legendary saxophonist

Marc Lamont-Hill (1978-present), professor and journalist

Marcus Mosiah Garvey (1887-1940), writer and activist

Margaret Bonds (1913-1972), composer

Maria Mutola de Lurdes (1972-present), legendary athlete

Mariah Carey (1969-present), legendary singer

Mariama Ba (1929-1981), writer

Marie Cecile Zinsou (1982-present), art historian and museum curator

Marie Van Brittan Brown (1922-1999), inventor of the CCTV system

Marie-José Pérec (1968-present), olympic champion

Marie Maynard Daly (1921-2003), biochemist

Mark Dean (1957-present), inventor and IT engineer

Mark Gordon Ella (1959-present), aboriginal rugby player

Marc Regis Hannah (1956-present), IT engineer and designer

Marius Tresor (1950-present), footballer

Marlene Dumas (1957-present), artist and South-African activist

Marshawn Lynch (1986-present), American football player nicknamed "Beast Mode"

Martha Louise Morrow Foxx (1902-1975), teacher and advocate for the blind

Martin Fitzgerald Lawrence (1965-present), comedian

Martin Luther King Jr (1929-1968), pastor, human rights activist, and martyr

Marvin Gaye (1939-1984), musician

Marvin R. Ellison (x-present), CEO of multiple big companies

Mary Jane Blige (1971-present), singer and actress

Mary Winston Jackson (1921-2005), astronaut, mathematician and engineer

Mary Eliza Mahoney (1845-1926), nurse

Mary McLeod Bethune (1875-1955), teacher and philanthropist

Mary Smith Peake Kelsey (1823-1862), teacher and activist

Mary Thomas (1848-1905), anti-colonialist rebel

Matthew Alexander Henson (1866-1955), explorer, first to physically reach the geographic north pole

Matthieu Kerekou (1933-2015), general and statesman

Maureen Nanawax Ayite (x-present), model, stylist

Maureen Watson (1931-2009), aboriginal writer

Maya Angelou (1928-2014), poet and activist

Maya Moore (1989-present), basketball legend

MC Solaar Claude M'Barali (1969-present), musician

Meghan Rachel Markle (1981-present), American actress, British royal and duchess of Sussex

Menelik Albert Tjamag (1970-present), musician

Merlene Ottey (1960-present), Jamaican athlete

Mervyn Bishop (1945-present), aboriginal photographer

Michael Clarke Duncan (1957-2012), actor

Michael C. Harvey (x-x), inventor

Michael Jackson (1958-2009), legendary musician, dancer, entertainer, producer and philanthropist

Michael Brown (1996-2014), martyr of U.S. police brutality

Michael Jerome Irving (1966-present), American football player

Michael Duane Johnson (1967-present), athlete and olympic champion

Michael Jeffrey Jordan (1963-present), basketball legend

Michel Aikpe (1942-1975), army captain and stateman

Michel Gohou (1959-present), comedian and actor

Michel Joseph Martelly (1961-present), musician and statesman

Michelle Obama LaVaughn Robinson (1964-present), lawyer and writer

Mick Dodson Michael James (1950-present), aboriginal lawyer

Mick Namarari Tjapaltjarri (1926-1998), aboriginal painter

Mike Procter Michael John (1946-present), South-African cricketeer

Miles Davis Dewey III (1926-1991), legendary musician

Milton Apollo Obote (1925-2005), statesman and leader of the independence fighters in Uganda

Mireille Dimigou (1986-present), writer and physical therapist

Miriam Benjamin (1861-1947), inventor and teacher

Miriam Makeba Zenzile (1932-2008), singer and activist

Miriam Tlali (1933-2017), writer

Mo Mohamed Muktar Jama Farah (1983-present), olympic champion

Modibo Keita (1915-1977), statesman, pan-africanist, first president of Mali

Moms Mabley Loretta Mary Aiken (1894-1975), comedian and actress

Monty Montgomery Eli Williams (1971-present), basketball coach

Morgan Freeman (1937-present), actor

Morris Chester Chestnut Jr (1969-present), actor

Mory Kante (1950-present), musician

Moshood Abiola Kashimawo Olawale (1937-1998), statesman

Muammar Khadafi (Al Gaddafi) (1942-2011), statesman, pan-africanist and martyr

Muddy Waters McKinley Morganfield (1913-1983), musician

Muhammad Ali (1942-2016), boxing legend and activist

Mumia Abu-Jamal (1954-present), journalist and activist

N

Nadine Gordimer (1923-2014), writer, activist and Nobel prize of literature

Naomi Campbell (1970-present), top-model and actress

Naomi Osaka (1997-present), tennis champion of Haitian and Japanese descent who lives in America

Nasir Bin Olu Dara Jones (Nas) (1973 - Present), musician

Nathan Nearest Green (1820-1890), distiller who formulated the legendary Jack Daniels whiskey

Nefertiti Neferneferuaten (1370-1330 BC), Egyptian queen

Neil deGrasse Tyson (1958-present), astrophysicist and educator

Nelson Mandela (1918-2013), legendary statesman, African icon and Nobel Peace Prize winner

Neville Bonner (1922-1999), aboriginal statesman

Neville O'Riley Livingston (Bunny Wailer) (1947-present), musician and legend of reggae music

Neymar da Silva Santos Jr (1992-present), footballer

Ngũgĩ wa Thiong'o (1938-present), writer

Nicolas Agbohou (x-present), writer and educator

Nikki Giovanni (1943-present), writer

Nikki Minaj (Onika Tanya Maraj) (1982-present), singer

Nina Simone (1933-2003), musician and activist

Nnamdi Azikiwe (1904-1996), statesman

Noel Pearson (1965-present), aboriginal lawyer and activist

Norbert Rillieux (1806-1894), engineer and inventor

Norbert Zongo (1949-1998), journalist and martyr

Notorious BIG (Christopher George Latore Wallace)

(1972-1997), legend of rap music

Noureini Tidjani-Serpos (1946-present), writer

NoViolet Bulawayo (1981-present), writer

Ntozake Shange (1948-present), writer

Nuruddin Farah (1945-present), writer

Nzinga (Anne Zingha) (1583-1663), queen of Mbundu in Angola

O

Obafemi Jeremiah Oyeniyi Awolowo (1909-1987),

statesman

Octavia E. Butler (1947-2006), writer

Octavia Spencer (1972-present), actress

Odell Beckham Jr (1992-present), athlete and American football player

Okot p'Bitek (1931-1982), writer

Olaudah Equiano (1745-1797), writer and abolitionist

Oliver Tambo (1917-1993), statesman

Olly Woodrow Wilson Jr (1937-present), composer

Olusegun Obasanjo (1937-present), general and statesman

Oodgeroo Noonuccal (Kath Walker) (1920-1993), aboriginal poet

Oprah Gail Winfrey (1954-present), TV icon, activist, actress, producer and philanthropist

Oscar Grant III (1987-2009), martyr of US police brutality

Oscar James Dunn (1826-1871), First African-American Lieutenant governor (Louisiana)

Oscar Leonard Carl Pistorius (1986-present),

Paralympian athlete, and convicted criminal

Oscar Palmer Robertson (1938-present), basketball legend

Ota Benga (1881-1916), slavery and human trafficking victim

Otis Frank Boykin (1920-1982), inventor and engineer with 28 patents

Otis Redding (1941-1967), musician

Oumou Sangare (1968-present), musician

Ousmane Sembene (1923-2007), writer and cineast

P

Panama Al Brown (1902-1951), boxer

Pascal Fantodji (1943-2010), thinker and statesman

Path McGrath (x-present), legendary stylist

Patience Asarebea Adow (1939-2005), politician

Patrice Emery Lumumba (1925-1961), statesman and martyr

Patrice Evra (1981-present), football player

Patrice Guillaume Athanase Talon (1958-present),

businessman and statesman

Patricia Era Bath (1942-present), ophthalmologist and inventor

Patrick Aloysius Ewing Sr (1962-present), basketball legend

Patrick M'Boma (1970-present), footballer

Patty Mills Patrick Sammy (1988-present), aboriginal basketball champion

Paul Belloni du Chaillu (1831-1903), zoologiste, anthropologist and explorer

Paul Hazoume (1890-1980), writer and politician

Paul Kagame (1957-present), former military leader, statesman and reformer

Paul Laurence Dunbar (1872-1906), writer

Paul Labile Pogba (1993-present), footballer and champion

Paul Revere Williams (1894-1980), architect

Paule Marshall (1929-present), writer

Paulinho Jose Paulo Bezerra Maciel Jr (1988-present), footballer

Pélé Edson Arantes do Nascimento (1940-present), football legend, best player of the 20th century

Percy Lavon Julian (1899-1975), chemist and inventor

Percy Pennington "Frenchy" Creuzot, Jr. (1924–2010), legendary culinary chef and philanthropist

Peter Abrahams (1919-2017), writer

Peter & Paul Okoye (P-Square) (1981-present), brilliant twin musicians and entertainers

Peter Tosh (1944-1987), musician

Patina Renea Miller (1984-present), actress

Petina Gappah (1971-present), writer and lawyer

Pharaons (x-x), rulers of ancient Egypt

Philando Castille (1984-2016), martyr of US police brutality

Philip A. Randolph (1899-1979), activist

Philip B. Downing (1857-1934), inventor

Philippe Noudjenoume (x-present), educator and activist

Phillip Emeagwali (1954-present), IT engineer

Phyllis Wheatley (1753-1784), former slave, first published black poet and writer in the USA

Phylicia Rashad (1948-present), actress

Pinckney Benton Stewart (PBS) Pinchback (1837-1921), first black governor in the USA

Prince Rogers Nelson (1958-2016), musician and producer

––––––––––––––––

Q

Quincy Delight Jones Jr (1933-present), legendary musician and producer

–––––––––––––––-

R

Rabah Madjer (1958-present), footballer

Rachidi Yekini (1963-2012), footballer

Ralph Ellison (1913-1994), writer

Randy Gene Moss (1977-present), legend of American football

Raoul Diagne (1910–2002), footballer

Ray Charles Robinson (1930-2004), musician ,

Razak Omotoyossi (1985-present), footballer

Rethices O. Fagbohoun (1985-present), technologist

Richard Allen (1760-1831), pastor and abolitionist

Richard Nathaniel Wright (1908-1960), writer

Richard Arvin Overton (1906-present), WW2 veteran and oldest living American at some point

Richard Pryor (1940-2005), comedian

Richard Spikes (1878-1963), inventor

Richard Wayne Penniman (Little Richard) (1932-present), musician

Richard Williams (1942-present), legendary tennis coach, dad of champions, businessman and activist

Rita Frances Dove (1952-present), poet

Rita Williams-Garcia (1957-present), writer

Riyad Karim Mahrez (1991-present), footballer

Robert Leroy Johnson (1911-1938), master guitarist

Robert (Bobby) Mellor Granites Jabanungga (Kantilla) (1946–1985), aboriginal actor

Robert Gabriel Mugabe (1924-present), statesman

Robert Nathanaliel Dett (1882-1943), composer

Robert Russa Moton (1867–1940), educator

Robert Sengstacke Abbott (1870–1940), lawyer and

journalist

Robert Smalls (1839-1915), abolition hero and statesman

Roberta Cleopatra Flack (Rubina Flake) (1937-present), musician

Roberto Carlos da Silva Rocha (1973-present), football legend and world champion

Roberto Enrique Clemente Walker (1934-1972), baseball player

Roger Arliner Young (1899–1964), zoologist

Roger Milla (Albert Mooh Miller) (1952-present), footballer

Roger W. Ferguson Jr (1951-present), CEO of TIAA, a large financial company

Romelu Lukaku Menama Bolingoli (1993-present), footballer

Ronaldo Luis Nazario de Lima (1976-present), football legend

Ronaldinho Gaucho (Ronaldo de Assis Moreira) (1980-present), football legend

Rosa Louise McCauley Parks (1913-2005), activist

Ruby Bridges Nell Hall (1954-present), children rights icon and activist

Ruby Dee Ann Wallace (1922-2014), actress, poet,

journalist and activist

Ruud Gullit (1962-present), football player

Russell Westbrook III (1988-present), basketball player

——————————

S

Salif Asalfo Traore (1979-present), musician

Salif Keita (1949-present), musician and activist

Sam Cooke (1931-1964), musician

Sam Nujoma (1929-present), statesman and first

president of Namibia

Samir Amin (1931-2018), brilliant economist and writer

Samora Machel (1933-1986), statesman and first president of Mozambique

Samori Toure (1830-1900), anti-colonial fighter and hero

Samuel Coleridge-Taylor (1875-1912), composer

Samuel Eto'o (1981-present), legendary footballer

Samuel L Jackson (1948-present), actor and producer

Samuel L. Kountz (1930-1981), brilliant surgeon

Samuel P. Massie Jr (1919-2005), educator

Sandra Bland (1987-2015), martyr of US police brutality

Sanite Belair (1781-1805), hero and martyr of Haitian resistance

Sarah Boone (1832-1905), inventor of the ironing table

Sarah E. Goode (1855-1905), inventor, first black patent recipient in the USA

Scott Joplin (1868-1917), composer

Scott W. Williams (1943-present), mathematician

Seaman Henry Gibson Dan (1929-present), aboriginal musician

Sefi Atta (1964-present), writer

Selma Burke (1900-1995), brilliant sculptor and educator

Serena Williams (1981-present), legendary tennis champion, designer and activist

Seretse Khama (1921-1980), statesman and first president of Botswana

Sero Kpera Gbodokpuno (x-x), king of Nikki in Dahomey

Shaka Kasenzangakhona Zulu (1787-1828), legendary zulu fighter, commander and emperor

Shaquille Rashaun O'Neal (1972-present), basketball legend

Sharice Davids (1980-present), congresswoman

Shelly-Ann Fraser-Pryce (1986-present), olympic champion

Sheryl Denise Swoopes (1971-present), basketball legend

Shirley Ann Jackson (1946-present), physicist and educator

Shirley Owens Alston Reeves (1941-present), singer

Shirley Chisholm (1924-2005), activist and politician

Shirley Franklin (1945-present), politician and former mayor of Atlanta

Shonda Lynn Rhimes (1970-present), writer and TV producer

Sidney Poitier (1927-present), actor and director

Silas Onoja (x-present), hyper-realist painter

Simone Biles (1997-present), legendary gymnast and olympic champion

Sloane Stephens (1993-present), tennis player

Smokey Robinson (1940-present), musician

Sojourner Truth (1797-1883), abolitionist hero and activist

Soni Oyekan (1946-present), chemist and inventor

Sundiata Keita (1217 - 1255), founder of the ancient Empire of Mali in Africa

Sourou Migan Marcellin Joseph Apithy (1913-1989), statesman

Spike Lee Shelton Jackson (1957-present), actor and director

St. Clair Lee (1944-2011), musician

St. Clair Drake John Gibbs (1911-1990), anthropologist and activist

St. Elmo Brady (1884-1966), chemist

Stella Ameyo Adadevoh (1956-2014), physician

Stephane Sessegnon (1984-present), footballer

Stephen Curry (1988-present), basketball legend

Stephon Xavier Marbury (1977-present), basketball player

Steve Biko Bantu (1946-1977), activist and martyr

Steve Broderick Harvey (1957-present), TV host and comedian

Stevie Wonder (Stevland Hardaway Morris Judkins) (1950-present), musician and producer

Sugar Ray Robinson (1921-1989), legendary boxing champion

———————————

T

T.J. Anderson Thomas Jefferson (1928-present), composer

Tafewa Balewa Abubakar (1912-1966), statesman and martyr

Taharqa (x-664 avant JC), legendary pharaoh, 690

to 664 BC

Taiye Selasi (1979-present), writer

Tamir Rice (2002-2014), martyr of US police brutality

Taraji Penda Henson (1970-present), actress and singer

Tayeb Salih (1929-2009), writer

Te Agbalin (x-x), founder of the kingdom of Hogbonou in Dahomey (current Benin Republic)

Teddy Pierre-Marie Riner (1989-present), legendary judo champion

Tedros Adhanom Ghebreyesus (1965-present), head of the World Health Organization (WHO)

Tegbessou Bossa Ahade (x-1774), king of Dahomey

Teju Cole (1975-present), writer

Tendai Huchu (1982-present), writer

Terrell Eldorado Owens (1973-present), American football player

Terrence Dashon Howard (1969-present), actor and singer

Terry MCMillan (1951-present), writer

Thabo Mvuyelwa Mbeki (1942-present), statesman

The Mills Sisters (Rita, Cessa, Ina) (x-x), aboriginal musician

Theodore Theopolis Jones II (1944-2012), judge

Theophile Obenga (1936-present), historian and egyptologist

Thierno Aliou Bhoubha Ndian (1850-1927), theologian and politician

Thierry Henri (1977-present), football legend

Thomas O. Mensah (1950-present), engineer and inventor

Thomas Mofolo (1876-1948), writer

Thomas Nkono (1956-present), footballer and legendary goalie

Thomas Sankara (1949-1987), visionary marxist statesman, reformer, military leader, and African martyr

Thomas Sowell (1930-present), economist

Thomas W. Stewart (1823-x), inventor

Thurgood Marshall (1908-1993), brilliant lawyer and US Supreme Court Justice

Tidjane Thiam (1962-present), brilliant executive and financier, CEO of Prudential and Credit Suisse

Tiemcoumba (x-x), African fighter for the French army

Tiger Eldrick Tont Woods (1975-present), legendary champion and greatest golf player of all time

Tiken Jah Fakoly (1968-present), musician

Tim Theodore Duncan (1976-present), champion and basketball legend

Tina Turner (Anna Mae Bullock) (1939-present), singer and actress

Tom E. Barlang Lewis (1958-2018), actor and aboriginal musician

Tommie C. Smith (1944-present), activist and

football player

Toni Michelle Braxton (1967-present), musician and actress

Toni Morrison (1931-present), writer, educator and Nobel literature prize winner

Tony Onyemaechi Emelulu (1963-present), economist, wealthy businessman and philanthropist

Tony Parker Anthony William Jr (1982-present), basketball champion

Toto Bissainthe (1934-1994), actress

Toussaint Louverture Francois Dominique Breda (1743-1803), military general, leader of the Haitian revolution

Tracy Chapman (1964-present), singer

Tracy Jamal Morgan (1968-present), comedian and actor

Trayvon Martin (1995-2012), martyr

Truganina (1803-1876), aboriginal leader

Tsitsi Dangarembga (1959-present), writer

Tupac Amaru Shakur (1971-1996), musician

Tyler Emmitt Perry (1969-present), comedian, actor and producer

——————————

U

Ulysses Kay (1917-1995), composer

Ursula Burns (1958-present), engineer, first black female CEO of a Fortune 500 company at Xerox

Usain Bolt (1986-present), legendary athlete, olympic champion and fastest human ever

V

Valentin Agon (x-present), researcher and agro-entrepreneur

Vanessa Diane Gilmore (1956-present), judge and writer

Venus Williams (1980-present), champion and tennis legend

Veronica Campbell-Brown (1982-present), olympic champion

Victor Anomah Ngu (1926-2011), inventor and educator

Viola Davis (1965-present), actress

Viola Irene Desmond (1914-1965), businesswoman

Virgil Abloh (1980-present), designer

Vivica Anjanetta Fox (1964-present), actress

Vivien Thomas (1910–1985), inventor

————————-

W

W.E.B. Dubois (1868-1963), writer and activist

Wallace Henry Thurman (1902-1934), writer

Walter E. Williams (1936-present), economist and educator

Walter Jerry Payton (1954-1999), American football player

Walter McAfee (1914-1995), inventor

Walter Mosley (1952-present), writer

Walter Anthony Rodney (1942-1980), historian, writer and martyr

Walter Max Ulyate Sisulu (1912-2003), anti-apartheid activist

Walter Sammons (1890–1973), inventor

Walter Scott (1965-2015), martyr of US police brutality

Wanda Sykes (1964-present), comedian and actress

Wangari Maathai (1940-2011), activist, tree lover and Nobel peace prize winner

Warren Hedley Williams (1963-present), aboriginal musician

Warren M. Washington (1936-present), famous meteorologist

Wesley Trent Snipes (1962-present), actor

Whitney Houston (1963-2012), legendary singer

Whoopi Goldberg (Caryn Elaine Johnson) (1955-present), actress, producer and TV host

Will Marion Cook (1869-1944), composer

Willard Carroll Smith Jr (1968-present), actor and musician

William Barry (1841-1915), inventor

William Grant Still (1895-1978), composer and pioneer

William Purvis (x-x), inventor

William Vacanarat Shadrach Tubman (1895-1971), statesman

Williams Wells Brown (1814-1884), writer

Willie Dixon (1915-1992), musician

Willie Hobbs Moore (1934-1994), physicist

Willie Mays (1931-present), baseball player

Wilma Glodean Rudolph (1940-1994), athlete and olympic champion

Wilton Norman Chamberlain (1936-1999), basketball legend

Window Snyder (1975-present), IT engineer and writer

Winnie Madikizela Mandela (1936-2018), activist

Wole Akinwande Oluwole Babatunde Soyinka (1934-present), writer and Nobel Prize winner

Wyclef Nel Ust Jean (1969-present), musician

W. A. Lovette (1867-x), inventor

Wynton Marsalis (1961-present), composer and trumpeter

————————

Y

Yaa Asantewa (1840-1921), Ghanian queen

Yaya Toure (1983-present), brilliant footballer

Yekini Yakhya Diop (1974-present), legendary wrestler

Yerry Fernando Mina Gonzalez (1994-present), footballer

Yewande Adekoya (1984-present), actress

Yewande Agnes Savage (1906-1964), inventor and physician

Youssou Ndour (1959-present), musician

Yvonne Adhiambo Owuor (1968-present), writer

————————————

Z

Zakes Zanemvula Kizito Gatyeni Mda (1948-present), writer

Zendaya Maree Stoermer Coleman (1996-present), musician

Ziggy David Nesta Marley (1968-present), musician

Zina Garrison (1963-present), tennis player

Zinedine Zidane (1972-present), brilliant footballer and coach

Zion Clark Shaver (1997-present), disabled but brave wrestler

Zognidi (Zoyidi), queen of Dahomey, wife of Guézo, mother of Glele, grandmother of Behanzin

Zora Neale Hurston (1891-1960), writer

Zumbi de Palmares (x-1695), Brazilian resistance fighter

A hero is a person dedicated to improving the world for the many. - Maya Angelou

We do not need to become heroes overnight. Just step by step. - Eleanor Roosevelt

Don't forget: you are the hero of your own story. - Greg Boyle

A hero is an ordinary individual who finds the strength to persevere and endure in spite of overwhelming obstacles. - Christopher Reeve

Books by Dallys-Tom Medali

- 1000 African Heroes (English)
- 30 Years of Painting and Drawing (English)
- Coming Back (English)
- Belles Poésies de Coeur and de Corps (French)
- Essais sur le Bénin (French)
- Héros Africains, Cahier de Recherches (French)
- L'Evangile Pratique (French)
- Le Manuel du Milliardaire (French)
- 10 règles du succès (French)
- Légendes Inédites d'Afrique (French)
- Perles and Pensées (French)
- Poisonous snakes in the Republic of Benin (English)
- Green Red and Blue (English)

http://www.dallystom.com
http://www.milliardaire.org
http://www.heroafricain.com
http://www.benindufutur.org

www.ingramcontent.com/pod-product-compliance
Lightning Source LLC
Chambersburg PA
CBHW031959080426
42735CB00007B/447